IT'S OKAY TO FEEL

Library of Congress Cataloging-in-Publication Data Available

ISBN: 978-1775143406

Published by Art Mindfulness and Creativity
www.artmindfulnessandcreativity.com

Feelings are natural. They come and go and constantly change. Part of being human is the ability to feel and express all of your emotions. Identifying your feelings, allowing yourself to feel, and dealing with them appropriately, is an important skill that needs to be recognized and developed. All of your feelings are okay. They are your feelings and you have the right to feel them. Allow yourself to feel, then choose the best way for you to deal with them.

This book is designed to help spark conversations with children around feelings and ways to express them. It can be read as a story or page by page while doing activities along the way.

For my daughter Ella, who helps me learn each day, and for all of the students I have taught throughout the years, I learn more from you then you do from me.

-AMC

I feel inspired.

What makes you inspired?

In what ways do your share your inspiration?

I feel ANGRY!

It is okay to feel angry. What makes you feel angry?

How do you deal with your angry feelings?

What can you do to express those feelings appropriately?

I feel energetic.

What makes you feel energetic?

How can you release your stored energy?

When you feel like you have too much energy in your body, what can you do?

I feel sad.

It is okay to feel sad.
What makes you feel sad?

What do you do when you feel sad?

What helps you feel better?

I feel grateful.

What do you do when you feel grateful?

Do you have a gratitude practice?

What are you grateful for in your life right now?

How does it feel to express your gratitude for something or someone?

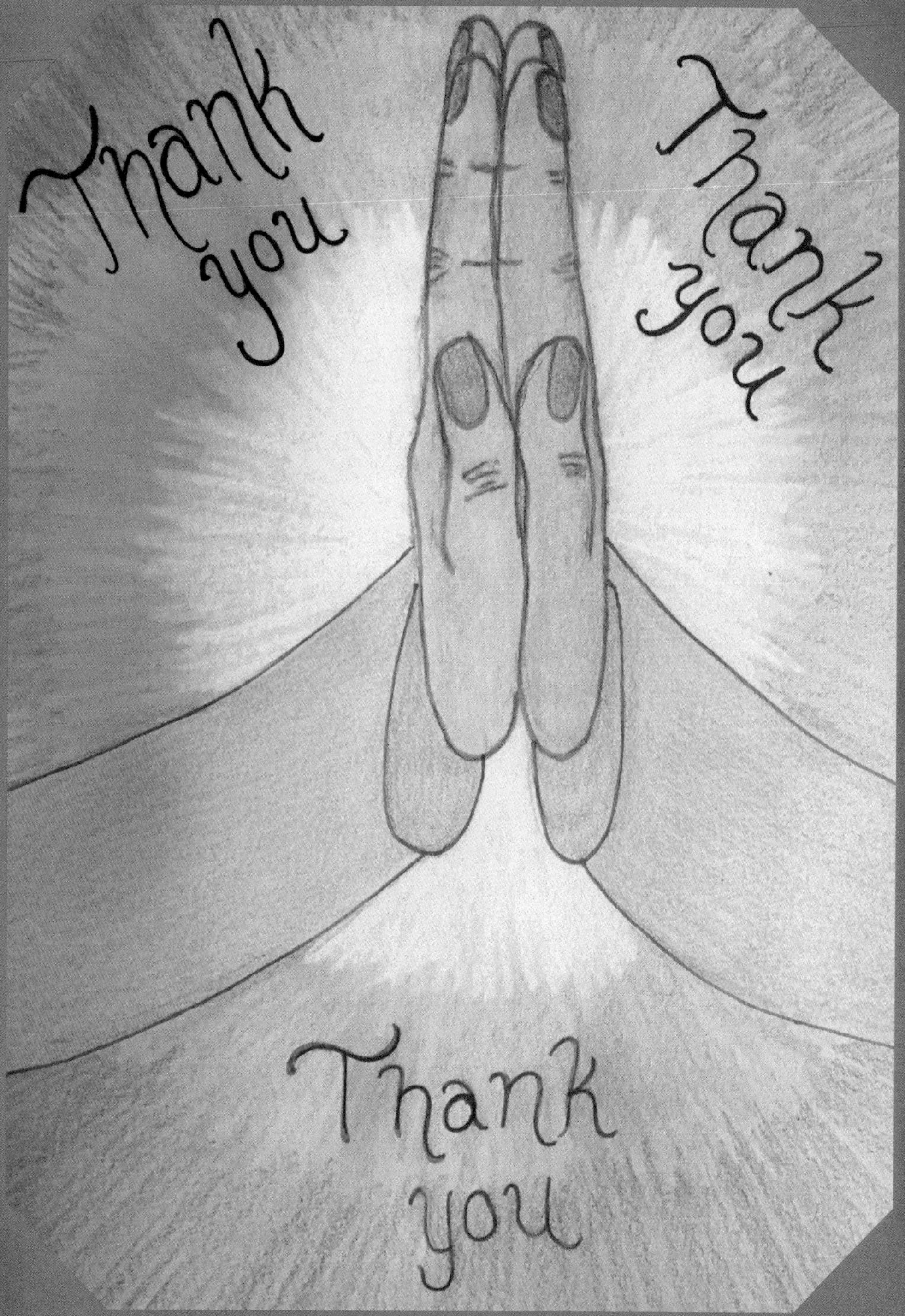
Thank you
Thank you
Thank you

I feel scared.

When do you feel scared?

What helps you get rid of your scared feelings?

What is behind the fear?

What steps can you take to overcome something you are scared of?

I feel affectionate.

Who do you share your affection with?

How do you express affection to others?

How do your acts of affection affect those around you?

I feel embarrassed.

What makes you feel embarrassed?

How do you deal with embarrassment?

What helps you move past an embarrassing situation?

How can you help others when they feel embarrassed?

I feel adventurous.

Where do you go when you feel adventurous?

What do you do?

Who do you have your best adventures with?

What parts of your body are most energized when you feel adventurous?

I feel vulnerable.

What situations make you feel vulnerable?

What do you do when you are in a vulnerable situation?

How can you overcome your vulnerability?

Who helps when you are feeling vulnerable?

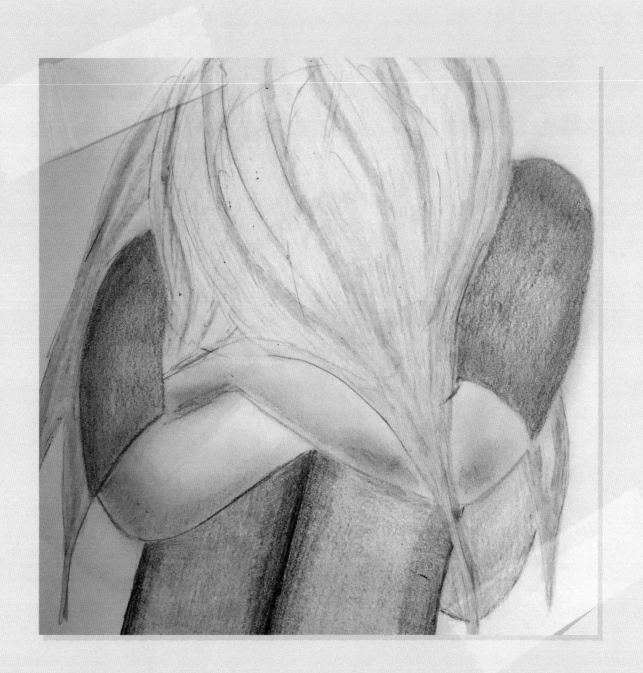

I feel peaceful.

What makes you feel peaceful?

Where do you feel peacefulness in your body?

How do you react to things when you are feeling peaceful?

How do others react to you when you feel at peace with yourself?

I feel desperate.

What situations make you feel desperate?

Where do you feel desperation in your body?

Who can you go to if you feel desperate?

I feel excited.

What types of things make you excited?

Where do you feel excitement in your body?

Who do you share your excitement with?

I feel confused.

What makes you confused?

Where do you feel confusion in your body?

Who can you ask for help when you are confused?

I feel joyful.

What brings you joy?

Who do you share your most joyful moments with?

How can you bring joy to others?

I feel relaxed.

What do you do to relax?
Where do you go?

Who do you relax with?

How does your body feel when you are relaxed?

How do you know when you need to take a break and just relax?

I feel anxious.

What does anxiety look like?

Can you show me with your body?

What are some situations that cause anxiety?

How can you ease your anxious thoughts?

I feel proud.

Have you ever been proud of yourself?

What makes you feel proud?

How can you share this feeling with others?

I feel jealous.

Is there anything you are jealous about?

What makes you feel jealous of someone?

What can you do when you are feeling jealous?

I feel creative.

What do you do to get your creativity out?

Are you a writer, drawer, builder, digital designer, actor, singer or musician?

There are so many ways to be creative.

Creativity helps feed your heart and soul.

I feel confident.

What makes you feel confident?

Can you think of a time when you were really confident?

What are some things you can do to build your confidence?

I feel loved!

Love is the strongest emotion of all . You can feel love for people, places, things, and yourself.

Who do you love and why do you love them?

It is also very important that you take time to love and care for yourself.

What do you love about you?

Teaching Ideas

Drawing: Get students to draw their own versions of the illustrations for each feeling.

Writing: Create a story about feeling monsters and how to deal with them.

Writing: Choose a body part to connect to a feeling and explain why.

Tableaus: Get students to create tableaus in small groups for each feeling.

Acting: Get students to silently act out feelings and get the rest of the class to guess which feeling they are portraying.

Acting: Choose a 'negative' feeling and create a play to help their friends when they are feeling that way.

About the Author

Amanda currently lives in Calgary, Alberta with her daughter Ella. They love to travel and go on adventures in the mountains together. Amanda teaches elementary school and has a Masters degree in Education. Her passions are drawing, creating, yoga and reading. She recently started a business called 'Art Mindfulness and Creativity' to help inspire others to find their own creative outlets.

www.artmindfulnessandcreativity.com

81820034R00029

Made in the USA
Columbia, SC
10 December 2017